Weekly Reader Books presents

Heroes of the Revolution

Abigail Adams

By Susan & John Lee

Illustrated by George Ulrich

CHILDRENS PRESS, CHICAGO

This book is a presentation of Weekly Reader Books.
Weekly Reader Books offers book clubs for children from
preschool to young adulthood.

For further information write to:
Weekly Reader Books
1250 Fairwood Ave.
Columbus, Ohio 43216

Library of Congress Cataloging in Publication Data

Lee, Susan
  Abigail Adams.

  (Heroes of the Revolution)
  SUMMARY: A biography of the parson's daughter who was
the wife of the second President and the mother of the sixth.
  1. Adams, Abigail Smith, 1744-1818—Juvenile literature.
2. Presidents—United States—Wives—Juvenile
Literature. [1. Adams, Abigail Smith, 1744-1818.
2. Presidents—Wives] I. Lee, John, joint author.
II. Ulrich, George. III. Title.
E322.1.A38L43   973.4′4′0924   [B]   76-47006
ISBN 0-516-04657-8

Martha Washington enjoyed having her to tea.

The Queen of England looked down on her.

Thomas Jefferson left his daughter in her care.

A member of Congress nicknamed her "Mrs. President."

Her husband called her "my dear partner." She called him "my better half."

Her name was Abigail Smith Adams.

Many people think of Abigail Adams as the wife of our second President. Others remember her as the mother of our sixth President. She was both. She was also an important person in her own right.

Abigail Adams wrote hundreds of letters during her lifetime. Many of these letters still exist today. They inform and delight readers now, just as they did 200 years ago.

The letters of Abigail Adams are rich clues to the past. They tell us about customs and habits during colonial times. They discuss events of the American Revolution. They give us a rare picture of day-to-day family life. Abigail's letters help us understand the history of our nation.

On November 11, 1744, a daughter was born to William and Elizabeth Smith. They named her Abigail. She was their second child.

Abigail Smith was born in the colony of Massachusetts Bay. At that time, there was no United States of America. The people didn't even live in states. They lived in one of 13 English colonies along the Atlantic Ocean. The King of England ruled these colonies.

Young Abigail never went to school because she was often sick. In those days, the law did not make children go to school. Besides, most colonists did not favor too much education for girls. Some even believed learning could harm a girl's mind!

The Smiths had no such ideas. Abigail needed an education. They gave her lessons to study at home.

Abigail was an eager pupil from the start. Her father was a minister. He made sure Abigail learned to read the *Bible*. She also read Shakespeare and other English writers. Reading history became her hobby. She even taught herself French.

Abigail became a good writer. She enjoyed composing letters. Writing letters taught her how to express ideas.

"I do not aim at entertaining," Abigail wrote to a friend. "I write merely for the instruction."

Abigail's letters were interesting, if not perfect. Her penmanship was poor. Some words were misspelled, others crossed out.

"Excuse this very bad writing," she once wrote. But there was nothing dull about the letters. Their author had a fresh, lively turn of mind.

Life was not all work and study. Abigail and her friends had lots of fun. They played games. They made dresses. They did needlework. They tried cooking new recipes. Sometimes, as a special treat, they visited nearby Boston.

Abigail also loved to visit her grandparents' farm. There, Grandmother

Quincy taught her to cook and sew. From her grandmother she learned good manners.

"I have not forgotten the excellent lessons which I received from my grandmother," she wrote many years later.

During her teens, Abigail began to have gentlemen callers. She liked John Adams best. He had been third in his class at Harvard. Now he was a lawyer. Like Abigail, he was well-read, outspoken, and interesting. Reverend Smith liked the young man, too. He agreed to let John Adams court his daughter.

Abigail Smith and John Adams were married in the fall of 1764. Her father married them. The wedding was a big social event in the town. The church was filled with friends and relatives.

The bride and groom went to live on John's nine-acre farm at Braintree. The house, made of brick and wood, faced the Old Shore Road to Boston. Across the highway rose Penn's Hill, with a view of the ocean. Behind the farm, the woods were thick with oak, maple, and pine.

The next few years were busy ones
for the couple. John had his law practice.
Abigail ran the house. The farm always
needed attention. Family and friends
dropped in. The days were filled with
work and fun.

John and Abigail became parents. They
enjoyed watching their children grow.
They talked about the right way to rear
them. There were many joys in their new
life together.

They both loved life in the country. But after several years, they decided to rent a house in Boston. John was tired of being away from home on business. Many of his law cases were in the city. They moved there in the spring of 1768.

Abigail felt like she had entered a nest of hornets. The colonists of Boston were in an angry, restless mood. The government in England had put a tax on glass, lead, paint, paper, and tea. The colonists now had to pay more money for these goods.

Public feeling against the taxes was high. The people of Boston would not buy English goods. Trade with England fell.

Abigail joined this peaceful protest. She did without English goods, too. The children wore homespun clothing. She stopped buying tea and served coffee instead.

King George was furious at his subjects in Massachusetts Bay. Didn't they know it was their duty to obey the law? The King sent English soldiers to Boston.

The soldiers brought nothing but trouble. They marched up and down the street outside Abigail's house. Abigail disliked the early morning drills. Often, she was awakened by the sound of drum and fife. Little Abigail and Johnny had to stay inside when troops were drilling in the square. Their mother did not want them playing outside with soldiers about.

After a while, things calmed down. England removed all taxes but the one on tea. The protests ended. Abigail relaxed. She thought the trouble was over.

Then, in December of 1773, three ships sailed into Boston Harbor with a cargo of tea from England. The colonists were outraged. Again, Abigail stayed away from shops selling English goods. Again, she put the teapot away and served coffee.

"The tea, that baneful weed, is arrived," she wrote to Mercy Otis Warren. "Great and I hope, effectual opposition has been made to the landing of it."

Days passed. The tea was not unloaded. Nor did the ships return to England.

The town was quiet. Too quiet.

Then, on December 16, a group of protesters met at the Old South Church.

Abigail stayed at home that evening. She tried to read. She paced the floor. Outside, the streets were empty. Suddenly she could hear shouting. She sent her cousin Will for news.

The news could only mean trouble for Massachusetts Bay. A group of colonists dressed as Indians had gone down to the harbor. There, they boarded the ships and threw every chest of tea into the ocean.

"Salt water tea," the citizens called it.

"A tea party," Abigail heard others say.

"Magnificent," was John Adams's feeling about the protest.

King George did not agree. Massachusetts Bay had set a bad example for the other colonies. The following June, the port of Boston was closed. No ships could go in or out. More English soldiers arrived in the capital.

John and Abigail decided to leave the city. Boston was no longer safe. Food and goods were already in short supply. In June they moved back to their farm at Braintree.

In August of 1774, John Adams left for a Congress at Philadelphia. Leading men from all 13 colonies would attend the meeting. They planned to discuss their problems with England. John Adams represented Massachusetts along with four other men.

"I must entreat you, my dear partner . . . to take a part with me in the struggle," he told Abigail. She gave him her full support.

"Your task is difficult and important. Heaven direct and prosper you. As for me, I will seek wool and flax, and work willingly with my hands . . . ."

Abigail Adams was now in charge of four little ones, the household, and farm. It was a hot summer, hard on the crops.

"We are burnt up with the drought," she wrote her husband, "having had no rain since you left us."

John missed the children. "The education of our children is never out of my mind," he wrote Abigail. "Train them to virtue."

Young Johnny answered his father. "I have been trying ever since you went away to learn to write you a letter . . . . Mr. Thaxter says I learn my books well. He is a

very good master. I read my books to
mamma. We all long to see you. I am, sir,
your dutiful son, John Quincy Adams."

The decision to leave Boston seemed a
wise one. "The Governor is making all
kinds of warlike preparations," Abigail
wrote her husband at the Congress. "The
people are much alarmed . . . ."

By Thanksgiving, John was home
again. Still, Abigail feared what the future
might bring. Over meals, at church, in the
marketplace, she heard the same talk. War
was on the way.

All winter long, the colonists got ready to fight. The men practiced marching and drilling. They hid powder and guns from the English.

On April 19, 1775, the uneasy peace ended. At Lexington and then Concord, English troops fought with local soldiers. England and her 13 American colonies were at war.

News of the fighting spread quickly from town to town. Troops from Braintree left at once to join the others. The Old Shore Road was thick with Minute Men.

Many soldiers stopped at the Adams's farmhouse to rest. Abigail cooked a stew. The children carried well water to the thirsty men. By nightfall, the barn was filled with soldiers, too tired to travel any further.

Several weeks later, John Adams returned to the Congress. He did not like leaving his family. Massachusetts was the heart of the war zone. Abigail was on her own.

"In case of real danger," he wrote his wife, ". . . fly to the woods with our children."

The danger was just beginning. One Sunday May morning, Abigail woke to the sound of warning drums and church bells. Minute Men were again hurrying down the Old South Road.

Another fight with the Redcoats was taking place. This time, English soldiers were raiding the countryside for hay. Minute Men fired at the troops to drive them off.

Abigail's kitchen was filled with soldiers in no time. She served them porridge and coffee. The men talked about their lack of bullets.

Then Abigail's brother saw her pewter
spoons. At once she put them into a kettle
to melt. Someone went for bullet molds.
Abigail was glad her spoons could help.

Little Johnny was proud of his mother.
"Bullet soup," he said, pointing to the
kettle.

"I suppose you have had an . . . account of the alarm we had last Sunday morning," Abigail wrote her husband. "Our house has been . . . a scene of confusion . . . . Soldiers coming in for a lodging, for breakfast, for supper, for drink . . . . You can harldy imagine how we live."

This raid was nothing compared to the battle one month later. On June 17, 1775, Abigail heard the thunder of guns at Boston. She climbed to the top of Penn's Hill with a spyglass. She could see hundreds of Redcoats. They were attacking the Americans on Breed's Hill.

"The battle . . . has not ceased yet . . . ." Abigail wrote John the next day. ". . . How many have fallen, we know not. The constant roar of cannon is so distressing that we cannot eat, drink, or sleep . . . ."

The English took Breed's Hill and then Bunker Hill. Boston was completely in England's grip. Without supplies, the suffering of those in the city got worse.

"As to Boston," she wrote later, "there are many persons yet there who would be glad to get out if they could . . . . No language can paint the distress of the inhabitants . . . . The bakers say, unless they have a new supply of wood they cannot bake above one fortnight longer . . . ."

Illness was a problem, too. "Tis a
dreadful time with the whole province.
Sickness and death are in almost every
family . . . . Our house is a hospital in
every part . . . . I should be glad of one
ounce of Indian root. So much sickness has
occasioned a scarcity of medicine."

As the winter wore on, Abigail ran short
of supplies. "Grain, grain is what we want
here . . . ," Abigail reported. "We shall
very soon have no coffee, nor sugar, nor
pepper, here . . . . not one pin to be
purchased for love or money . . . . linens
not to be had at any price."

In March, the colonists met with
success at last. General George
Washington was now head of the

American army. His troops surrounded
Boston. The Redcoats were trapped. Their
only escape was by water.

Within two weeks, all the English
troops sailed away. Abigail watched the
retreat from the top of Penn's Hill.

"To what quarter of the world they are
bound is wholly unknown; but 'tis
generally thought to New York," she wrote
John.

Boston was once more in colonial hands.

By summer, the representatives in Congress were ready to break away from England. Thomas Jefferson, a representative from Virginia, was chosen to write a Declaration of Independence.

John Adams wrote his wife about the events of July 2, 1776: "Yesterday, the greatest question was decided which ever was debated in America . . . . A Resolution was passed without one dissenting Colony 'that these United Colonies are, and of right ought to be, free and independent States' . . . ."

A week later, Abigail took the children to Boston. She wrote John about the holiday:

"Last Thursday . . . I went with the multitude into King Street to hear the Proclamation for Independence read and proclaimed . . . . Colonel Crafts read from the balcony of the State House . . . . Great attention was given to every word . . . . The bells rang, the privateers fired . . . and every face appeared joyful."

The long months alone gave Abigail an independence of her own. She got used to making her own decisions. She was raising four children and running a farm by herself.

She wrote John: "And, by the way, in the new code of laws which I suppose it will be necessary for you to make, I desire you would remember the ladies and be more generous and favorable to them than your ancestors. Do not put such unlimited power in the hands of husbands."

Abigail was ahead of her time with other ideas. She was against slavery," . . .

those who have as good a right to freedom as we have." She believed in education for both sexes. She was sorry "female education is neglected," and made sure young Abigail learned along with her brothers.

The war with England continued. But Massachusetts was no longer in danger. Most of the fighting was taking place in other colonies. John Adams was still in Philadelphia, busy as President of the Board of War. Abigail ran the farm herself.

In 1779, Abigail and John began their longest separation. Congress picked him to make a peace treaty with England. He left for Paris with his two older boys in November. Abigail stayed home.

It was three years before England and the United States agreed on a peace treaty. At last, the two enemies came to terms. The treaty was signed September 3, 1783. The colonies had won their independence!

The end to war made travel safer. In the summer of 1784, Abigail and her daughter sailed to Europe. John had a house near Paris ready for their arrival. They were happy to be together again.

Abigail wrote her friends all about life in France. Paris was "the very dirtiest place I ever saw." The French people, ". . . from the gaiety of the dress and the places they frequent, I judge pleasure is the business of life."

Abigail needed eight servants to keep the house going. She and John had important people over to dine every week. They enjoyed many guests, among them Thomas Jefferson and the Marquis de Lafayette.

John and Abigail were invited to dine at the homes of other officials. At one such dinner, Abigail admired the rich table. "The dessert was served on the richest china, with knives, forks, and spoons of gold," she noted.

The first time she saw a ballet, Abigail was "shocked." After a while, she got used to young dancers showing their "garters and drawers on stage."

The following year, John Adams became his country's first minister to England. As minister, he would represent the new United States. In the summer of 1785, the family moved to London. They did not expect a warm welcome.

Part of Abigail's job as a minister's wife was meeting the King and Queen of England. She soon presented herself at Court. She told her sister all about it:

"We were placed in a circle round the drawing room, which was very full, I believe two hundred persons present . . . . when the King comes in, he takes persons as they stand . . . . he has . . . a red face and white eyebrows . . . . The Queen was in purple and silver. She is not well shaped nor handsome . . . . but don't you tell anybody that I say so . . . . I never expect to be a Court favorite. Nor would I ever again set my foot there, if the etiquette of my country did not require it."

Abigail enjoyed her stay in London anyway. She saw a famous actress in *Macbeth.* Again, as in Paris, the theater shocked her. "Much of Shakespeare's language is so uncouth that it sounds very harsh," she wrote home.

She took a tour of Windsor Castle. She visited Westminster Abbey and heard a concert of Handel's music. She visited old buildings of the Saxons and Normans at Winchester.

Abigail's children added to her happiness. She wrote son John, back in Massachusetts studying for Harvard. She and John witnessed the marriage of their daughter, Abigail. In 1787, they became grandparents. Busy as she was, Abigail Adams cared for Thomas Jefferson's daughter while she was in London.

But John and Abigail were homesick. In 1788, John Adams asked to be replaced as minister to England. They sailed for Boston in April.

Their farm had to wait. Instead, home for the Adams family became New York City. In 1789, John Adams was elected the first Vice-President of the United States. It was his duty to preside over the meetings of the Senate of the United States.

Abigail enjoyed public life. She made new friends easily. She met the President's wife:

"I took the earliest opportunity to go and pay my respects to Mrs. Washington. She received me with great ease and politeness. I found myself much more deeply impressed than I ever did before their majesties of Britain."

In time, Abigail Adams and Martha Washington became close friends.

In 1797, John Adams was himself elected President of the United States. The nation's capital was now at Philadelphia, while the new one was being built.

America's second First Lady was busier than ever: "At 5 I rise. From that time till 8

I breakfast, after which till 11 I attend to my family arrangements. From 12 until 2 I receive company, sometimes until 3. We dine at that hour . . . . After dinner I usually ride out until 7."

In 1800, Washington D.C. became the nation's permanent capital. John and Abigail moved into the new mansion called the President's House.

Abigail described it to a friend: "The house is upon a grand and superb scale, requiring about 30 servants to attend and keep the apartments in proper order . . . . The river, which runs up to Alexandria, is in full view of my window, and I see the vessels as they pass and repass. . . . . but there is not a single apartment finished

. . . . We have not the least fence, yard, or other convenience, without, and the great unfinished audience-room I make a drying room of, to hang up the clothes in. The principal stairs are not up, and will not be this winter."

On January 1, 1801, the first New Year's reception was held in the President's House. The President and Mrs. Adams received guests in the beautiful oval room. Foreign officials wore their best powdered wigs and shiny swords. The ladies came dressed in gowns of silk and velvet. How far they had come from the days before independence!

In 1801, Thomas Jefferson replaced John Adams as President. It was time for John Adams to retire from government. He and Abigail returned to a new farm at Quincy, Massachusetts.

Abigail loved their new life together. ". . . I have commenced my operations of dairy-woman;" she wrote a friend, "and [you] might see me, at five o'clock in the morning, skimming my milk."

To her son, she wrote: "You will find your father in his fields, attending to his hay-makers . . . . The crops of hay have been abundant . . . ."

Abigail's old age was filled with joy. She
saw her oldest son become the Secretary of
State under President Monroe. She played
with her grandchildren and great-
grandchildren. Her partner and husband
of 54 years shared many happy memories
with her.

She wrote her friend, Mercy Warren: "So long as we are inhabitants of this earth and possess any of our faculties, we cannot be indifferent to the state of our country, our posterity and our friends . . . . We have passed through one revolution and have happily arrived at the goal . . . . we have our firesides, our comfortable habitations, our cities, our churches and our country to defend, our rights, privileges and independence to preserve."

The United States won independence because of strong people like Abigail Adams. During the Revolution, she raised four children, ran the family farm, and aided American soldiers. She shared the duties of public life with her husband. She continued to educate herself throughout life.

Luckily, Abigail Adams left a record behind. Because of her many letters, the past is less of a mystery today. Through these letters, her life and times still live.

About the Authors:

Susan Dye Lee has been writing professionally since she graduated from college in 1961. Working with the Social Studies Curriculum Center at Northwestern University, she has created course materials in American studies. Ms. Lee has also co-authored a text on Latin America and Canada, written case studies in legal history for the Law in American Society Project, and developed a teacher's guide for tapes that explore women's role in America's past. The writer credits her students for many of her ideas. Currently, she is doing research for her history dissertation on the Women's Christian Temperance Union for Northwestern University. In her free moments, Susan Lee enjoys traveling, playing the piano, and welcoming friends to "Highland Cove," the summer cottage she and her husband, John, share.

John R. Lee enjoys a prolific career as a writer, teacher, and outdoorsman. After receiving his doctorate in social studies at Stanford, Dr. Lee came to Northwestern University's School of Education, where he advises student teachers and directs graduates in training. A versatile writer, Dr. Lee has co-authored the Scott-Foresman social studies textbooks for primary-age children. In addition, he has worked on the production of 50 films and over 100 filmstrips. His biographical film on Helen Keller received a 1970 Venice Film Festival award. His college text, *Teaching Social Studies in the Elementary School*, has recently been published. Besides pro-football, Dr. Lee's passion is his Wisconsin cottage, where he likes to shingle leaky roofs, split wood, and go sailing.

About the Artist:

George Ulrich grew up in Massachusetts and graduated from Syracuse University in New York. He is a popular illustrator of educational materials and children's books. George lives with his wife and two sons in Marblehead, Massachusetts.